TABLE OF CO

Digital Nomads, Long-Term Budget Travelers & Expats: The Ultimate Guide

Dedication

Foreword

Knowing yourself to know where to go

10 Travel Hacks useful before you board.

10 Travel Hacks to use during your trip

EXTRA BONUS - The obvious idea you are not using

30 Travel Hacks for Digital Nomads and Expats

Resources to make your life abroad easier

From the same author

Endnotes

DIGITAL NOMADS, LONG-TERM BUDGET TRAVELERS & EXPATS: THE ULTIMATE GUIDE

50 Tips, Tricks, Hacks and Ways to Free Stuff & Cheaper Flights in a Practical Guide to Travel Plans

Levi Borba

2020

Copyright © 2020
All rights reserved

"Difficulties strengthen the mind, as labor does the body."

LUCIUS ANNAEUS SENECA

For all who went through complications in 2020

FOREWORD

What if I told you that there is a way to win free flight upgrades, money to spend as you wish, and even a night in a five-star hotel?

What if there is one single secret to save you thousands of dollars in the next time you travel for a longer period?

Do you know there is a trick to pay even less when flying with low-cost airlines?

Those years working in the world's best airline and travelling to over 50 countries across every corner of this planet taught me one thing:

There are so many ways to save money while travelling that people would be shocked at it.

Living abroad for almost a decade also made me learn a few things about personal security (especially after being robbed by very creative thieves), how to adapt to new environments, avoid unnecessary problems by using a simple word and how to fit living costs to your budget (no matter what your budget is).

After years working in the airline sector, I moved to the tourism & accommodation industry. There I discovered that hotels and hostels are willing to give many things to guests for **free,** only if they follow a popular Brazilian motto:

Para rir, primeiro você tem de fazer o outro rir ("To laugh, first you need to make others laugh"). To understand what it means and how this advice can result in great perks, you can jump directly to hack 3 in the last section of this book.

In the next pages, I will share 50 of the best life-saving, money-sparing hacks I learned. The first part are for all travellers, be it for short or long term. The other thirty are for *explorers, digital nomads* and *expatriates. In other words*, individuals leaving home for longer periods.

If you read my previous book (*Moving Out, Living Abroad and Keeping your Sanity - 11 secrets to make your expat life better than you imagine*), you already learned those universal principles which skyrocket your adaptation and allow you to enjoy a fascinating international life. This book differs considerably from the previous one. If *Moving Out* was about the way to not lose your mind with the cultural shock and quickly ace the local life, here I present a plethora of jam-packed **practical** hacks and streetwise tips.

Things I learned while being robbed in Athens, warned by a cop in the Middle East, after an accident in the Carpathian Mountains or in a 5-star hotel in Istanbul (where I stayed for free). Tips and methods I recommend to the clients of my consulting firm (www.expatriateconsultancy.com)

Hope you enjoy it!

KNOWING YOURSELF TO KNOW WHERE TO GO

As the title of this book makes explicit, our hacks will bring the greatest advantages for three types of people:

- Travellers
- Digital Nomads
- Expats

Still, those not included above can also profit from the ideas in the next pages.

To make clear the difference between those 3 given types, let me delineate what we understand for each:

- Travellers: People spending time far from their homes. For example, backpackers taking sabbatical periods from their universities/work to make international trips. Sometimes they survive with their economies, sometimes doing volunteer work in exchange for accommodation, but rarely they work in remunerated jobs (otherwise they would fit in the two next categories). There is a discussion if tourists are also travellers or not, especially among backpackers, who boast themselves for getting off the beaten path (as if this was a medal-worthy achievement).

In my view, anyone keen to explore a land they are not familiar, is a traveller. That includes some tourists.

- Digital Nomads: The Digital Nomads (or *DN*s), just like the backpackers, usually stay for months or even years away from their origins. The biggest difference here is they perform remunerated work. Nowadays there is a growing variety of jobs done remotely and online: digital marketing, ghostwriting, language teaching, online commerce, and software development are just some examples. So while building their reputation, those modern nomads also travel from one place to another, favouring locations with good connectivity, network possibilities, and the most important: a low cost of living. Just imagine a person providing digital marketing for an Australian company and earns an Australian salary but lives in Thailand, paying just a fraction of the living costs of Melbourne.

- Expats: Just like the digital nomads, the *expats* also live abroad and do paid work. Unlike the DNs, they are less of a visitor and more of a resident. They are not living where they live just because of the lower living costs or good networking, but because of something unique the country offers to them. This unique factor can be a great career opportunity, a move to build a family in a more favourable environment, among others. The range of jobs executed by expats much wider than those of DNs, not restricted to online services but extending to areas like hospitality and industry.

It is normal that at some point you will change between those 3 types. I was once a traveller, now an expat. I know people that lived like a *DN* until they had a reason to put roots in the country where they previously would stay just for a few months. The classification above is not static, but still important. By knowing what you are, you get closer to understand what are your goals.

The understanding of one's targets is essential to not fail in an international assignment, be it as an expat, *digital nomad,* or any other sort. To take your goals as a life vest during difficult moments is one fo the universal principles I explained in my previous book (*Moving Out, Living Abroad and Keeping your Sanity*). As I promised, this book will be more about practical, nuts and bolts solutions for your life abroad.

Time to take the first step and crack the code.

10 TRAVEL HACKS USEFUL BEFORE YOU BOARD.

1 – THE VPN AND INCOGNITO MODE TO HAVE BETTER PRICES

Those are two hacks in one (which means this book has actually more than the 50 promised in the cover, even though you paid just for fifty. Sweet deal, right?). For this reason, it may take a few pages.

During years, I worked in an airline department named *Revenue Management*, or as we called it: RM. In this area are the gentlemen responsible for the (apparently insane) variations of air ticket prices. Even though for the consumer those movements may look chaotic, they obey a myriad of mathematical rules, geographical variables, and real-time information. Dozens of analysts incessantly input additional information in the model and specialists responsible for entire regions calibrate the precision of the systems with only one thing in mind:

Sell those seats for the right price.

But…

What is the right price?

The answer may look vague, but after years in RM it just

comes automatically:

It is the maximum price the consumer is willing to pay.

To explain how we calculate it takes days and is beyond the scope of this book - and I am almost sure all the contracts I signed prohibit me from doing so. During the last years of my airline career, I was training new specialists, and it took two days only to explain the logic behind the calculations. What I can guarantee is one thing:

Those *right prices* differ between countries (or, as we called, POS–*Point of Sale*). The maximum price a middle-income customer from a country like Bolivia is willing to pay for a certain flight is logically different (probably smaller) than the willingness to pay for it from a Los Angeles higher-income customer.

Therefore, it is common airlines having, for exactly the same flight, different prices depending on where you are from. Few years ago there was a scandal in Brazil when people realized that switching the language of the reservation page of an airline changed drastically the price.

Now, not always change the language will work. Sometimes they will define your country by your frequent flyer profile or credit card. For those cases, this hack will not work. However, often airlines determine the country of the passenger by the *IP (Internet Protocol)*

So, here comes our first hack: **Try a VPN to book your ticket**.

VPN stands for *Virtual Private Network* and is a way to change your IP for another location. If you are booking a flight from the

USA to Mexico, and live in California, try comparing the prices while using a VPN that changes your IP to Mexico. Just take care to use a protected and safe network to not have your card information stolen.

Besides the IP, there is another way for airlines to change their prices to unfavourable conditions for you: the cookies stored by your browser. Don't be fooled by their sweet names, those files serve a not so tasty purpose: airlines can use it to check how many times you searched on the internet for the same ticket. The more you search, the more they know you *need* it. So, they can increase the price in the next time try to quote it.

A trick to avoid it is even easier than using a VPN. You just need to do one thing:

Do not allow your browser to denounce you.

To do that, it is enough to activate the *incognito* mode of your browser, which avoid the cookie tracking by websites. *Voilà!* With *Incognito* mode, you became *invisible* to them. Now you can search the ticket combination you want, as many times as you wish, without the airline increasing prices just because they know how badly you want to fly during those specific days.

2 – ASK YOUR HO(S)TEL WHAT YOU WIN IF YOU BOOK DIRECTLY

Websites like Booking.com, Hostelworld, Expedia, etc are what we call *OTAs (Online Travel Agencies)*. When you book accommodation with them, the amount you pay doesn't go entirely to the hotel. Those OTAs take a share. 15% is their usual cut.

As a hospitality business owner, it is painful to see how much those websites take in commissions, while simultaneously they do little for the guest.

Therefore, any lucid hotel or hostel manager will be glad to offer you a discount if you book directly via their website or by phone. 5% is a safe value, but would not be absurd to ask for a 10% discount. If you are a *Digital Nomad* travelling frequently, that 5% to 10% discounts can become a considerable sum in one year.

The best tactic is to call the accommodation you want before doing the reservation and ask for this possibility. It is even better if you ask it together with the sweetest phrase a Hotel

Manager can hear (in the last section of this book I will detail it).

3 – SHORT-CONNECTING FLIGHTS CAN AWARD YOU AN UNFORESEEN PRIZE. STOPOVERS, TOO.

There are two types of flights: direct and connecting flights. The meaning of the first is obvious, while the second are those where you stop in one or more airports before your destination. Sometimes you wait on the plane, but in most cases, you need to leave and change to another aircraft. In this change lives our trick.

Normally, the minimum connection time (MCT) is regulated by law and varies according to each airport (usually bigger airports have longer times since the passengers may need to walk more to change planes). For example, Frankfurt Airport has an MCT of 45 minutes. The best way to discover is to search on the internet for *MCT*+[name of the airport].

What happens when you book a flight, the airplane has a delay because of atmospheric conditions or mechanical problems and you arrive at the connecting airport with less time than the MCT to change flights?

According to the firm Claim Compass[1] you can earn up to 600 euro if your flight delays to the point you miss the MCT. This is valid for any flight departing from the European Union, independent of the carrier. Other countries like the USA or Australia have their own rules, which is also worthy to check.

However, it is essential to stress that this rule is valid only when you buy the connecting flights in a single reservation. In other words: when the airline offers you a connecting-flight and they cannot land in time for you to make the connection. If you try to buy two separate flights to create an artificial short-connection, the compensation rules do not apply. They also do not apply if the airline delivers you in time and you miss your flight because you were walking around the duty-free shops, needed to go to the toilette, etc. So while using this hack, you must be aware that the sweet-prize for the delay compensation mentioned above is just valid when the airline delays their flights, not you delay your steps.

There is another possibility: Book flights with very long-connections (near or over 24 hours) or stopovers. Some companies (like Turkish Airlines[2]) offer free hotel stays and city tours so their passengers don't need to wait an entire night at the airport. Last time I flew with them, my flight from Brazil arrived in Istanbul in the evening and my next flight, to Europe, departed only in the next afternoon. So they offered me a free transfer to a five-star hotel, with dinner and breakfast included. All in an *economy class* ticket. An unbelievable bargain.

Unfortunately, this is not a common practice among airlines. Still, always worthy to check what they offer for long connections & stopovers.

4 – HAVE 3 SEATS FOR YOU BY BOOKING JUST 2.

In my last trip back from South America to Europe, my wife and I still had two flights separating us from home. The first was over 12 hours long, and we really could use some extra space to stretch our legs while watching a movie.

In those situations, everyone's fear is a quarterback-sized man sitting at your row and squeezing you like a toothpaste. For a 12 hour flight, this is a spooky panorama.

My wife is more of a window passenger, while I prefer the aisle. This is when we came with a simple and very intuitive idea: One of us chooses the window and the other the aisle in the same row. In a not-so-crowded flight, it was unlikely someone would select the middle-seat with so many others available.

This is not a guaranteed hack because if the plane is almost full, someone may just choose whatever is free, even if it is the middle seat between you and your partner. However, virtually all the times I made this in not-so-crowded flights, it worked well.

5 – TAKE ADVANTAGE OF THE FLIGHT IMBALANCE.

This is a very interesting trick I learned during my years working at airline headquarters.

When a big event (like the Super-Bowl or the Olympics) or a special holiday (like Carnival in Brazil) approaches, airlines dedicate extra flights to those destinations, and touristic companies organize charters. They do it because there is demand and people are willing to pay more. For those wanting to travel for big dates, tickets can be pricey.

However, there is something called "flight imbalance", which gives to date-flexible travellers a significant advantage.

To understand it, first we need to know that every time an aeroplane is flying, it creates costs for the airline. Considerable costs like fuel, which may represent near 40% of all company expenses. Therefore, an aircraft must have as many passengers as possible to offset the costs of the very act of flying (and spending fuel).

Even for higher prices, it is easy to sell a ticket to travel to Brazil for carnival. It is also easy to sell a ticket to the host city of the Olympics just one day before the opening ceremony. So, even for higher prices, the extra-flights and charters fly crowded on the way to there. But an airplane will rarely stay grounded in the airport during the entire Olympics or carnival, so they usually fly back to their original bases.

That is what we call *Imbalanced*: a flight with an enormous demand in one way, but minimal demand on the way back.

Since one passenger is better than no-passenger, to avoid planes coming back empty, airlines offer great deals and special prices in the opposite direction. There is where your opportunity lies.

Example: The Venice Carnival of 2019 started on 16 of February. Airlines and tourism companies offered flights to the Italian city departing from all over Europe. You can expect a salty price to go to Venice during Carnival. On the other hand, a flight departing from Venice on 16 or 17 of February can have very low prices, because the number of people willing to fly *out* of the city during the carnival is not even near the number of people flying *into* the city. To not have empty aircrafts returning, airlines offer discounts.

Bottom line: If your location is hosting a big event (sports, conferences, etc) or have a special holiday, chances are that traveling out from your city during this day (and return to your town when everyone is leaving it) will save you a considerable amount of money.

6 – RESEARCH PRICES OF LOW-COSTS AIRLINES SEPARATELY

There is one common knowledge for any traveller: Google Flights and aggregators like Skyscanner and Kayak saves us time. Those websites compare the prices of dozens, sometimes hundreds of airlines in a matter of seconds.

However, people would be surprised by what they don't do (or at least not efficiently) and the opportunities they waste. Especially when flying with low-cost airlines.

A good part of the low-cost carriers, like Ryanair, Wizzair or EasyJet, operates in a system called *Point-to-point* network. Legacy carriers (airlines that are not low-cost) like Lufthansa, Emirates, British Airways, and others operate in a *Hub and spoke* network. This means low-cost companies often sell tickets to fly from a city to another with no stop in between, while legacy carriers have stops called *hubs* (like Lufthansa have in Frankfurt or Emirates in Dubai).

How this can save you money and why is this related to Google Flights and other aggregators?

The explanation lies in how you search for a ticket on the internet. Most people will search for the price from the place where they are departing to where they want to arrive.

Therefore, if you are planning to travel from Warsaw to New York, you can enter in Kayak or Google Flights and look for flights departing from WAW airport to JFK (for example). It will show to you plenty of options, and currently a round trip between those two cities cost around 430 euros in the cheapest option, with one or two stops in the way.

However, while I write this book, there is a way to go from Warsaw to JFK for 285 euros.

But Google Flights and most aggregators are not showing it anywhere.

Why?

The answer is simple: Those websites do not work well with low-cost airlines.

In the case mentioned above, the cheapest way would be to go to Norway with one of the two low-cost carriers flying from Warsaw to Oslo. From there, take another low-cost flight to New York.

Google will not show you that because low-cost airlines work in a *point-to-point* system, as I mentioned above, remember? They are not optimized to sell flights with a stop in the way. But if you create this stop by purchasing two separate tickets, you can find much better prices.

The best way to find those low-cost opportunities is to look for flights separately. When I want to travel from Poland to Brazil, I don't look for flights departing only from Warsaw, but also Barcelona, Milan, London, Frankfurt, etc. If there are cheaper flights from Milan or Frankfurt to Brazil, then I just find a low-cost airline to go from Warsaw to there and from there to Brazil. In this way, you will perform a low-cost hack that even Google couldn't find!

Just be aware that flying with low-cost carriers brings its challenges, like the need to pay even for a cup of tea or coffee. But for the cost-savvy, it is a treasure.

7 – FORGET ABOUT FLYING ON MONDAYS AND FRIDAYS.

Airlines (and later, hotels and sports events) are very good at one marketing method: Customer segmentation. They delineate their commercial strategy all over the expected behaviour of their customers. They spend millions in research to profile and project the behaviour of people buying tickets every day. This entire effort starts with a very basic level, where all the passengers are grouped into two major categories: Business or Leisure. There are other groups (like pilgrims or visiting relatives) but their relevance is minor compared to the previously mentioned.

Business passengers are usually not paying their own tickets, they buy with less anticipation and are relatively inelastic (meaning they don't care much about the price). On the other side, leisure customers plan their trip well in advance, pay their own tickets, and are more price-sensitive (or elastic).

Business travellers tend to fly at the beginning of the week, like Monday, and return before the weekend, especially Friday. Meanwhile, they rarely travel on Sundays (except in the Middle East, where this is a working day) and Wednesdays.

Because of the lack of corporate travellers, airlines typically price Sundays and Wednesdays at lower rates than Mondays and Fridays. There are exceptions, though. If a certain destination is attractive, for example, for Saudi nationals, Sundays can be expensive since this is a working day for them. Special events and holidays also can inflate the prices of specific days. However, all the rest being constant, the best opportunity to save money is to avoid flying on Mondays and Fridays.

8– FOR LOW-COST AIRLINES, ONE WAY MAY BE THE WAY

One of the main tools an airline has to avoid flight imbalance (see hack number 5) is to stimulate the customers to buy round-trip tickets (tickets from A to B and then the way back, from B to A). In this way, they avoid people flying outbound and then taking a different airline to fly back. They stimulate round-trip tickets by offering better prices for them in comparison with buying two one-way tickets.

However, low-cost airlines are not worried about flight imbalance like legacy carriers. They have smaller aircrafts rotating among multiple destinations. Therefore, to sell one-way tickets is not a problem for them.

This creates a great opportunity to enjoy the flexibility of building your own itinerary by travelling with one-way tickets and hopping from one country to the next one. There are even few situations where buying two one-way tickets with low-cost airlines will be cheaper than one round-trip!

9 – MAKE YOUR SUITCASE EASY TO FIND

This hack is straightforward, but still so many people will read and think:

I cannot believe I never realized that before!

Yes, the same happened to me. My first dispatched luggage was just a big, dark-coloured, plain bag. We were landing at Ezeiza, Buenos Aires, an airport where baggage carousels are the same for multiple flights and hundreds of bags. Having a bag similar to so many others, I guarantee one thing:

It is not cool to take the luggage of someone by mistake and see the person rushing to you thinking you are stealing!

Avoid this kind of embarrassing situation with a simple trick. A trick that will also help others to not take *your* luggage. A single method to make easier complaining to the airline if they miss your bag. After all, what are you going to answer when the airport employee asks you:

What details can we use to identify your luggage?

Put a big sticker on it!

It can be one of your favourite destinations, of your garage band, or just some random abstract pattern.

This will work very well if the material of your luggage is hard, like acrylic or plastic. But if it is fabric, then a sticker may not stick long enough. In this case, the best recommendation is to just buy a bag with some shocking, weird, or fluorescent colour.

It may not look perfect to an Instagram photo, but will save you time and avoid losing your stuff in those ever-growing airports.

10 – LAST-MINUTE TRAVEL

This is the last of the hacks to use *before travelling* in this book. It is also, by far, my favourite.

This single piece of advice saved me money while guaranteeing that I visited some incredible places for prices fitting perfectly an economical budget. Here it goes:

Do *Last-Minute* travelling.

You may think I mean the impulsive trips made by young backpackers who buy their tickets a few days (or less) before boarding. It is not exactly that, although with the same *surprise* factor.

There is a growing number of websites selling last-minute travel packages. Some of them belong to airlines, some to travel agencies. Examples are the German tourism behemoths TUI and Lufthansa with their own last-minute websites[3][4]. There are also plenty of independent sites, specialized in packages like *On The Beach*, from the UK, or *Holiday Guru*, which is available in European countries like Spain, Austria, Switzerland, etc.

Where I live I use *Wakacje*[5], a Polish website offering complete packages with flight included or just accommodation. I used them a few times already.

Especially in the last part of the warm season (September and October), the number of offers on those websites is so big that you will always find an excellent opportunity. The packages are from hotels ranging from economic to full-service five stars. You can expect discounts from 40% to 80%. A week in a four-star hotel on a Greek beach with flight included can cost less than the flight itself in a normal situation.

The apparently inconceivable opportunity comes with a single condition: You must depart in the next days after buying it. Sometimes, literally the next day!

This condition may look like a big NO. After all, how is it possible that people with a job and responsibilities will schedule a holiday for *Tomorrow*?

The truth is that you don't need to do it only a few days before flying! My wife and I have the following approach: She schedules her days off, while I inform my assistant I will be out in the next month, let's say, from the second to the third week.

We already have our holidays scheduled. We just do not know yet to *where*. Therefore, when the dates scheduled for our holidays approach, we navigate last-minute websites looking for offers to travel in the chosen days (usually in the next 48 to 96 hours). We decide between pleasant options, like a villa at Morocco, a resort in the Black Sea, an urban hotel in Italy, or a boutique B&B in Malta. We *always* found something for incredible prices, in a suitable destination and, the best part:

With a stimulating ingredient of surprise!

10 TRAVEL HACKS TO USE DURING YOUR TRIP

1 – DO NOT RELY ONLY ON YOUR WALLET OR PHONE BATTERY

One of the most convenient things about modern travelling is the possibility to carry less paperwork. A hundred years ago, besides carrying a relatively heavy passport, the absence of visa-free travelling also made mandatory to bear extra documents.

Now you can carry virtually all those documents (except the passport) in electronic form. Instead of cash, you can use a card, phone, or even smart watch. Instead of a train or plane ticket, you are free to use a QR code on the screen of your phone. Those innovations save time and reduce some weight in your hand luggage. However, they bring an additional risk:

What if your battery finishes?

Not always you will have a power bank or a charging plug nearby. A cautious train-ticket checker or public office employee can make it difficult to overcome a situation where documents are missing because there is no battery. I saw few times other travellers needing to pay fines or leave the wagon because the ticket purchased by phone was not visible because of low-charged battery.

This is the reason I am an enthusiast of having a Plan B. If a train inspector is in front of you, asking for your ticket and the battery of your phone is dead, you should be able to give him an alternative to check.

You can either go old-school and print it, or just e-mail it to yourself and save it in a tablet or any other electronic device. Problem solved, and the Plan B saved you.

Regarding e-mail documents, what I will tell now is a potential lifesaver:

Before long-trips, always scan all your documents (passports, visas, IDs, etc), and email the images to yourself. In the case you are stolen, robbed or just miss everything after a rough night, this can be your way back into normality. It will also avoid you to get stranded in a country or, even worse, at an airport.

Few years ago, I spent an entire day locked in an airport terminal in Doha because someone stole my documents in Athens, Greece. Although I had my newest passport with me, the previous passport contained my visa and the thief took it. I could not pass immigration, so after an entire day waiting and sitting, they sent me back to Europe.

Not a day to remember, but a lesson learned. So scan your essential documents before travelling and e-mail them to a safe (and accessible) location.

2 – SPREAD THE WORD OF YOUR BIRTHDAY (OR HONEYMOON)

Sometimes you can get surprised about the extra mile that some hotels and hostels go to please their guests (and gather a good review). Things like giving perks during special dates. Here I am talking as a Hostel-owner (everyone invited to check it if you visit Warsaw) too: If you share with us that this is a celebration date for you, we will try to make it special.

Last year part of our honeymoon was in a coastal city in Brazil called Florianópolis. The place was lovely, and we choose a hotel just in front of the beach. Unfortunately, this hotel was quite popular (it has an excellent value for service, being inexpensive and simultaneously amazingly located) so I couldn't reserve a room with a beach view.

Few weeks before check-in, I sent a message to the reception that we would be glad to spend our honeymoon in their hotel. We hoped it could be memorable.

Yes, this was the whole content of the message. I didn't ask for *anything* extra. I just informed them it was an important occasion for me. Arriving at the reception, again I quickly mentioned it was our honeymoon. The receptionist gave us our key and showed us our room.

That is when the surprise came: We had this fabulous sea-view, even though we just reserved a room with a street view. Every morning we could see the sailboats arriving and departing with the turquoise background of the Atlantic Ocean. Splendid.

Not always the hotel will give you an extra so memorable just because it is your honeymoon or anniversary. Sometimes they have nothing to give. However, it costs you nothing to try, and eventually, you may have a positive surprise.

3 – USE THE POWER OF A GOOD REVIEW

Independently of the business, there will always be a combination of words which, when said by customers, sound enchanting. For bartenders, it can be "you can take all the change", for mechanics it may be "do what you need to do and my insurance will cover", while for real estate agents it is something like "my wife loved the house you are selling!".

For hoteliers, it is "I would love to do a great review of your Hotel and mention your name, can I?".

Frequently guests underestimate how powerful are the reviews made in websites like TripAdvisor, Booking, Google Maps, etc. For a Hotel, an average grade lower or higher than the competition can be the difference between bankruptcy and success. For a receptionist, a bad or good review can trigger a warning or a promotion. Those few minutes spent writing your review may generate long discussions and performance evaluations.

I say that by my own experience.

There were days when a bad review of my Hostel impaired my mood the whole morning, while an excellent review made me smile for hours.

With this in mind, next time you stay in a hotel, try to use this charming phrase and see the magic happen (do not be surprised if you win a free drink or a bottle of wine):

I would love to do a great review of your Hotel and mention you by your name, can I?

4 – APPS TO HELP IN A COMMON EMERGENCY

To write an entire section in a book about how to find a toilette may sound laughable, just until you really need to go *vroom*. Or to find yourself in a huge line in a crowded place. Here in Warsaw, in the Old Town, there are chemical bathrooms with the appearance of a murder scene (except that it is not blood on the floor). Sometimes is preferable to just hold it until be back home or in a shopping mall.

I thought that too until I went to one of those free walking tours to know more about the historical side of the city. To my surprise, besides explaining monuments and palaces, the guide also gave us a priceless information: one of those historical buildings had a free, spacious, and incredibly well-maintained public bathroom.

My jaw dropped. Years of living in this city and I never knew about it!

The good news is that you don't need to go to walking tours of each city to know about the secret loos (although free walking tours are a great program on a sunny day). Few apps are doing this job for you, revealing the nearest restroom in a matter of minutes.

One of them is *SitOrSquat*, offered by the toilet paper brand *Charmin* (how convenient!). Apparently, most of the cities available are in the United States. Users can rate the toilette with *sit*, which means a well-kept WC, or *squat*, meaning it is not a place to go back.

Unfortunately, *SitOrSquat* is not updated frequently, different from our second recommendation, *Flush*. With the information about WCs in many European cities, they have over 190 thousand restrooms in their database and even allow you to search offline.

With such precious resources, you will not need to pee in a dark alley and risk a €10,000 fine, like happened with a 19-year-old boy in Italy[a].

5 – HAVE A DUMMY WALLET (AND TAKE CARE WITH SELFIES)

In a few countries, like (unfortunately) the one I came from, pickpocketing crimes are commonplace, not an exception. This is particularly true in touristic regions and famous landmarks.

Experienced travellers should be smart enough to not carry enormous volumes of cash. Still, pickpocketing is painful since our wallets also carry documents and cards. If you follow the hack number one of this chapter, you will not lose completely your identity, but still will waste time to re-issue lost IDs and passports.

This is the reason I recommend having a dummy wallet when visiting risky regions. By risky I mean places like:

- Commercial walking streets in Brazil, like the 25 de Março in São Paulo or the Saara in Rio de Janeiro.

- Omonia; in Athens, Greece. (Where I was stolen).

- Around the Fontana di Trevi in Rome (be aware of groups of young boys).

- Gare du Nord in Paris.

- Las Ramblas in Barcelona (My wallet survived Las Ramblas, but my sunglasses disappeared.).

When preparing your dummy wallet, always consider that criminals are bad, but not stupid. Therefore, your dummy wallet needs to look real.

- Put some expired cards in it so it looks stuffed.

- Put some money (bills and coins).

- Place it in your back trouser pocket.

Be aware that I **do not** recommend you to have a dummy wallet with the purpose of saving money. Having a wallet with no cash represents an additional risk. A robber, for example, may come back asking for the money not found or just for revenge.

For places like I mentioned above, besides your wallet, other expensive gadgets like cameras or cell phones can be mugged. The best moment for street criminals to take them is when you are taking selfies.

Visualize with me: you are posing, your arm far away from the rest of your body, concentrated on looking good for Instagram. Thieves come riding bicycles and with a quick slap in your arm, take it from you and escape in their bikes. There will be *no chance* to reach them. You lost.

The scenario above is especially true in crowded places and

walking streets, so they can mingle with the rest of the pedestrians.

Avoid exposing your expensive camera or cell phone for a selfie in packed places. Not only you can be a target for crooks, but it is also annoying for other people to wait for your arm/selfie-stick to get out of the way for them to keep walking.

6 – A BLAZER FOR A FLIGHT UPGRADE

Even though a business seat occupies a space equivalent to 2/3 seats in economy class, the regular price for them far compensates it. Therefore, airlines keep selling them. However, they are also harder to sell.

Now imagine how much waste of potential is to have no one using those marvellous high-tech oases, the big-screen inflight entertainment, the complimentary Italian lotions available, and fancy dishes. In the airline I worked, they even warmed your nuts (no double meaning intended).

Airlines also know that flying with an empty seat in business class is a waste. After all, many of the greatest airlines in the world build their reputation with this compartment.

For this reason, they frequently upgrade passengers.

On my very first international trip, still at university, my friends and I got upgraded. If you were had the same luck, maybe you also got puzzled:

Why did they choose me?

It is easy to explain why you didn't get an upgrade. For example, if you are travelling with a sizeable group it is unlikely they will upgrade everyone or just part of it.

On the other side, reasons to move a passenger to a better class are plenty. Below some I saw during my airline career:

- Customer with a high-tier frequent-flyer program card (like Platinum for United Airlines or Sapphire/Emerald at OneWorld alliance).

- Celebrities

- People with a disability or special conditions.

- Well-dressed people, chosen randomly by the cabin-crew.

If you are not a high-spending, frequent-flyer member or not famous enough to be on talk-shows, probably you ignored the first two points. The last one, on the other side, is within your reach. Still, so few people know about it.

On the occasions where you saw a steward invite a man in the next row to business-class, there is a possibility she chose him because of the good-looking suit. The chance to have the same privilege using dreads and tie-dye shirts are negligible unless you are a reggae-star.

Get suited-up to win an upgrade. The worst that can happen is to attract some flirting eyes from the person in the next row.

7 – GET RID OF YOUR COINS AT THE AIRPORT

It is a common hobby to collect money from all over the world. My mom shares this interest, and for this reason, I frequently bring her some change from my trips. However, you do not need to have 10 of the same Ethiopian birr, Albanian lek or Laotian kip coins. Still, this is most likely to happen if you bring coins back home.

To handle paper bills of exotic currencies, exchange houses charge large spreads (the difference between the real rate and what they charge you). If you try to exchange coins, chances are the cashier will laugh and call the next in line.

Therefore, unless you want to keep those coins for the rest of your life (or until the next visit to Addis Abeba), better just give them to some passer-by. Or spend them at the airport. In the first case, you win a *thank you,* in the second some overpriced souvenir to give to your mother-in-law.

8– TAKE A CAB AT THE DEPARTURES SESSIONS

It is fine if you saw the title above and thought:

What a prehistoric stuff! Who takes cabs in those times of rideshare apps?

I would think the same but dozens of countries don't have access to ridesharing applications. Denmark, Saudi Arabia, or Bulgaria, for example. Because of market conditions or by government regulation, chances are in some point you will be in a situation when your phone will not bring a driver in a few clicks. You will need to take a cab to leave the airport.

Our natural impulse is to walk out of the arrivals terminal and choose a driver from a bunch of taxis waiting at the door. Even this being the most convenient way, it is not the cheapest.

A simple trick is to not take any cab in the arrivals, but go up and take it at the departures level of the airport. Taxis bringing people to departure leave the airport empty, which is a waste of time and fuel for them. Therefore, there is a big possibility they will offer you a better rate than the taxis in the arrivals area.

You save money and time just by taking the stairs.

9 – THE WAY TO AVOID THE INCONVENIENT RECLINER

There is an apocryphal story of a torture method used by ancient Chinese, where a restrained person has droplets of water dropped in hiss forehead until becomes insane. Most likely, they called it Chinese just to give it an aura of mystery, and likely the real creator was the medieval Italian lawyer Hippolytus de Marsiliis.

Despite the questionable origin of the idea, I found a useful adaptation of it to avoid one of the most inconvenient passengers in economy class: the recliner. To be more specific, I refer to people who sit right in front of you (in any means of transport), reclining their seats while you are trying to eat your inflight snack. Eventually, they cause accidents like a stain of wine on your shirt or coffee in your pants.

I will tell you a secret now.

Few people can resist a constant flow of cold air directly in their eyes or forehead. The air conditioner exit above your seat is usually adjustable. When the annoying recliner moves his seat in your direction, do the following:

1. Close all the other air exits the seats at your side (if the person doesn't mind). Since every exit shares the same airflow, closing the others strengthens your flow.
2. Direct your air exit to the head of the person who reclined and is almost laying on your lap.
3. Open it. Let the full-force cold-air cannon hit the cumbersome individual mercilessly.

Now you can eat in peace.

10 – NEVER USE THE BATHROOM GLASS CUPS TO DRINK

Hotels rated as three-stars or above often have those two glasses at the side of the washbasin. The whole idea is to replicate a homely environment, where those glasses are used to the morning mouth-wash. Usually, they look crystal clear, but…

Have you ever thought about how they clean it?

First, I want to warn you about one thing: Hotels do not always clean the glasses after each guest. If the room maid came and saw them in exactly the same position and not dirty, she will just leave it. *The principle of the least effort* works here.

Now imagine that after every flush with the toilet lid open, thousands of dirty-water droplets float all over the room. Philip Tierno, a microbiologist at New York University, says that aerosol plumes can reach as high as 15 feet (4.57 meters)[12]. Even looking spotless, some toilet droplets felt in those glasses if someone flushed with an open lid.

Let's be more optimistic and suppose the previous guest touched the glasses and used it, so the room cleaning service cleaned it.

What do you imagine she uses to clean those cups? Do you think they use a proper dishwashing detergent? If the room doesn't have a kitchen, there is absolutely no reason for a cleaner to carry dishwasher, together with all the other things in their heavy carts. She will use any other chemical product she has. Window-cleaner, for example.

Bottom line: if next time staying in a Hotel you want to risk using the glass cups, at least you know where the smell of ammonia comes from.

EXTRA BONUS - THE OBVIOUS IDEA YOU ARE NOT USING

Carry local currency?

Depending on how popular the country you are visiting is for travellers, it's difficult to exchange money upfront in your homeland. As much as finding a place to buy Turkish or Czech currency is common in a country like Poland, it may not be a rule for i.e. Ethiopian birr.

If half of your country is going on holidays to Bulgaria and the other half pack their cars to spend lovely weeks in Croatia, local exchange houses are likely to offer your currency there. Even better: with rates similar to those in your own country. Why would you carry a 2-week pile of banknotes if you can exchange the exact amount of money after arrival only when needed and if needed?

Do a small research and ask your friends who went there last year. In this case, most likely you do not need to prepare a supply of cash and put yourself at risk of losing a wallet or being stolen.

On the other side, in relatively undeveloped places like Tanzania or Laos, you may find exchange houses only at airports and similar places. I know rates are unfavourable, but who wants to stay with no money at all, while there is so much to see?

The situation changes if you plan to visit a pretty raw and undiscovered location. Let's take a closer look at a few journeys we made not so long time ago.

We did once a round trip at Balkans and passed through Bulgaria, Serbia, and Romania. The first part of our holidays went smoothly (as described above) - we crossed Bulgaria with a pocket full of Lev and arrived in Serbia needing to buy Dinars.

It quickly turned out that both countries, despite sharing a border, rarely exchange each other currencies. This surprise repeated when we came to Romania and remained with hundreds of Dinars that no one wanted to buy.

We underestimated the fact Serbia is still a relatively isolated country and tourists from farther countries are still a surprise – although I recommend to you as it's a beautiful place and full of history. When planning your budget, take into consideration the political situation of your destination and neighbouring relations.

Let's move for a second to one of the most visited places in South America, Iguazu waterfalls. Its location is near the triple border of Brazil, Argentina, and Paraguay. It must be full of exchange houses since hundreds of people are daily crossing the border (be it to sightsee, work or shopping), right?

Well, that's what we thought, but we couldn't be more wrong.

Iguazu is a small city in Argentina. It turned out even the bus station, with dozens of daily departures to Brazil, doesn't have a single exchange house. Moreover, many shops accept only cash. This put us in an awful situation. We lost hours searching for a place that accepted dollars and a bit of a good mood as well.

These situations taught me that when possible, walk the extra mile and find an exchange house at home to buy some exotic currency, even if sometimes it seems like you don't need it.

Be smart with money when you know enough about the

country you are visiting. Be cautious when you don't and check beforehand how to exchange it. I used to be more an "exchange at the destination" person, while my wife prefers to do it before travel.

Speaking honestly with you, the author's wife wrote this bonus chapter, and she likes to remind him about this mistake. Yes, hello – it's me talking. Don't make me remind you about it too.

30 TRAVEL HACKS FOR DIGITAL NOMADS AND EXPATS

1 – PHONEMIC LANGUAGES AND THEIR SECRET

When you are planning to spend a longer period in another country, learning the local language brings a myriad of benefits.

I. If English is not widespread there, learning the local language will facilitate eating, drinking and hanging out in the same places as the locals. With better prices.
II. Service providers that are worldwide famous for ripping-off foreigners (mechanics and taxi drivers, for example) will think twice before scamming you.
III. It will be easier to socialize with locals, and also to understand if anyone says something about you in parallel.
IV. To understand and grasp the literature, music and local culture will help you learn what to say or not. Learn what to do or not and the daily idiosyncrasies.

Those are only some pros of learning the idiom of your new country. In my book *Moving Out, Living Abroad and Keeping your Sanity - 11 secrets to make your expat life better than you imagine* there is an entire section clarifying how speaking the local dialect will escalate your performance in any country.

In this hack, however, I want to teach you one thing to make this learning easier and (much) cheaper.

If the language you want to study is phonemic, you don't need to pay a language school!

Unless you are a language geek, probably it is the first time you hear the word *phonemic*. *Phonemic* languages are those where the written letters match most of the sounds (phonemes) when we speak. Languages like Spanish, Italian, Finnish or Polish are very phonemic. In those, you can trace almost every spoken sound to a letter representing it.

Probably you can guess the least phonemic among the major western idioms. The one where the letter representing a sound often depends on the context and changes between distinct words. The language where to do an elementary school dictation sounds like a nightmare.

It is French.

Learn French at home is a challenging task. Unless you have plenty of possibilities to practice speaking and listening, chances are that you will learn how to write and read, but the pronunciation will be flawed. This is because French is not phonemic, letters have many alternative pronunciations (occasionally we do not pronounce them at all). At this point, a professional teacher can help you correct the way you speak and train your listening.

Contrarily to French, it is possible to learn phonemic languages like Italian, Spanish or Polish at home without major harm to pronunciation. Polish is considered one of the hardest

European languages, and I learned it studying only at home by using a tool called *Lingq*[1]. It took me three years to reach a conversational level on it, approximately the same time that I would spend in a language school with regular classes. The time is the same, but the difference is how much I paid. A monthly subscription of Lingq costs around 10 euros. A language school would cost 12 times more. What I paid for one year learning online, I would spend for a month in a regular school.

The best part: I studied when it was more convenient, like during my lunchtime at work or in the metro going back home.

Wspaniałe![2]

2 – THE CHEAP AND THE BEST

If you move abroad under the sponsorship of a multinational company or as part of government staff, perhaps you will not need to worry about this hack. Your employer should provide the support you need to win the battle against bureaucracy.

However, if you moved out just like me, years ago, you will need to find few experts to help you. Not all of them immediately, and not all of them separated from each other, but at some point, you will look for:

- A sworn translator, to translate documents from your original language and validate certificates in your new country.

- An immigration specialist or lawyer, to help you renew your visa or do your first residence permit.

- A business lawyer, to help you incorporate your company, in case the country has complicated rules.

- An accountant, especially if you pay tax or have significant tax-returns.

- A babysitter, an investment advisor, a car dealer, a healthcare plan, etc.

I cannot count how many times I saw people tricked or plainly cheated when using these "professional services". I also fell into a trap once.

But why do so many people fall in the hands of scammers and bad professionals?

The answer is straightforward: Because they always choose the cheapest alternative.

This is what happened to me:

Just after arriving in Poland, I looked for an immigration specialist to help me handle the residence permit application and opening a company as a foreigner.

I received the offer of an excellent immigration assistance office in Warsaw that could help me for a little more than 4 thousand zlotys. A few days later, a competitor offered to do the same service, but for less than three thousand.

I chose the cheapest and regretted it later. She didn't help me with anything, but still charged me few thousand zlotys and threatened legal action. So besides paying this "immigration lawyer" that solved nothing, I still needed to find one to deal with my bureaucratic problem.

Months passed without solving my problem. I needed to cease my contract with her, lost the money paid and hired the other office that made an offer months before. This one had a higher price, but they solved the issue.

If I did not choose the cheapest at first, I would have saved a considerable amount of money and time.

The same applies to countless other expats. They get ripped off and deceived by (apparently) professionals with artificially low-prices that later show their actual face.

By no means I am advising you to go for the most expensive option. I am also not saying low-price is equal to low quality. This is not always true. What I am saying here is to use other factors to take a decision, not only price. A bad immigration lawyer or translator can create losses much bigger than what you would save by hiring the cheapest.

I saw many people getting in complicated situations by choosing disappointing and low-grade assistance. So, I started a consultancy specialized in pipelining the best professionals to expats needing them, and for a better price.

Even if you do not use our services (we have a superb blog too, for free[10]), it is worthy to remember: It is your life at stake. Hiring the cheapest option can make you waste more than you would save by few orders of magnitude.

3 - HAVE AN ESCAPE PLAN ALWAYS READY

This is a sensible point. Most expats prefer to not even think about it. Eventually, it happens and they try to solve it *ad hoc*, even though this can cost multiple times more than if they planned earlier.

I am talking about the moments when an emergency happens and you need to leave the country immediately, in a matter of hours.

It could be because of a beloved relative passing away in your fatherland.

It could be the fault of a quick change in the sociopolitical environment.

Or even because of an epidemic state like the one happening right now, while I write this book, with the COVID-19 spreading everywhere.

Independent of the reason, you should know how to fly (or move) away as quickly as possible, if needed.

In my case, I know that if a major situation arises, before 14:00 every day, I can buy a flight in the later afternoon to Amsterdam and from there to Brazil. There is also an alternative via Paris, and both would allow being on the other side of the planet the next morning.

Designing an escape plan has a positive collateral effect: You also notice prices to buy last-minute tickets. By that, you can discover interesting promotions. For example, I discovered weeks ago that last-minute tickets to my country are at promotional prices during specific periods.

Establish your escape route and have it in mind for when an emergency materializes.

4 – GO BEYOND REGULAR MEDIA IN YOUR RESEARCH

If you read my previous book (*Moving Out, Living Abroad and Keeping your Sanity*), you probably remember the tragicomic story of Breno. For those unfamiliar, he was a colleague from the times I was living in Qatar. He gave up after a few weeks there, all because his expectations were completely unrealistic. Breno arrived to Doha (the Qatari capital) imagining something like a smaller Dubai, with plenty of nightlife, parties, fun, and a relatively laid-back lifestyle. After facing a completely different (and less fun) reality in Qatar, he left.

There are thousands of Brenos around. Maybe millions. People that moved to other countries after getting information only from biased and unreliable sources.

I can't emphasize enough how important is to do a decent research before moving, and I am sure most digital nomads and expats do it. Unfortunately, not everyone does it right.

Resort to the easiest sources, like newspapers and internet portals, is not a good idea. Journalists are not there to help your life abroad, but to earn their salaries. They may create content only to draw attention. For this reason, sensationalism and exaggeration happen. The difference between what the press portrays and the reality of the streets can be abysmal.

So if I am telling you that the main media vehicles are not the best source to research before moving abroad, where should you seek information?

The answer is: *from the real people*. People who went through the same experiences and endured it for years.

Thanks to the same *internet* I criticized above, you can reach them easily.

In Social media, there are plenty of groups named like "Foreigners in [name of the place]". I do not recommend them as the sole source of information since many of their members are recent arrivals, still in their honeymoon phase. Even not being the most reliable, it is already better than traditional media.

The real deal is to look for groups of locals, and there are two simple ways to do it.

The first way is to look for common interests. Before coming to Europe, I joined local groups about entrepreneurship, football, and history. Three subjects interesting to me. While discussing stimulating things, I learned about local views on those subjects and other topics. Sometimes, when you are surrounded by other foreigners, you feel not knowing enough about where you are living. For those cases, enrol in a course or to volunteer activities can be useful and pleasant.

The second way is to find language learning groups in your new hometown. If you live in a large city, chances are that there are plenty of them organized via social media. Besides learning how to communicate with locals and explore their idiom, you can also offer to teach them your language. This opens a great window for socialization and meeting interesting people.

5 – IF YOU NEED A CAR, THERE ARE CREATIVE ALTERNATIVES

Before jumping into the subject of buying a car, a minor disclaimer: not always you need one. While living in South-America or Middle-East, to have a car (or live with someone who has one) is inevitable in some cities, here in Eastern Europe it is not really a *must*. At least not in the main cities, and not for most of the people.

However, in some places, it is nearly essential. Previously I mentioned the Middle East. while living there, in Doha, there was still no underground/subway available. The excruciatingly hot temperatures for three quarters of the year and the common absence of sidewalks turned walking into an unpleasant adventure. Therefore, going to work by car was inescapable for me. I entered an arrangement with my flat mate where I paid for part of his fuel, and he took me to and from work. To go to other places I used ride-sharing applications.

The monthly expenditure in this arrangement was far less than the cost I would bear if I bought a car. Especially because I was not doing long car trips, but only to downtown or to the airport. Therefore, even the taxi fares were small.

If you don't have a flat mate to do this kind of deal, there are still alternatives to save you a considerable amount of money.

The first one is to count on ride-sharing apps and taxis. In Chile, I could go walking to my work and public transport was easily available, as in Poland. So, when I needed a car, I called a driver using any phone app. Since my usage was sporadic, the expenditure was smaller than the price of car insurance, for example. If you are not a frequent-driver, odds are that you will save money by using ride-sharing apps like *Bolt, Lyft,* or *Uber*.

The other alternative is to just rent a car.

When you rent instead of buying a vehicle, you will have a series of benefits that most expatriates forget:

- Not paying insurance, since the rental company is responsible for it.

- Not paying for bureaucratic procedures like document transfers or inspections.

- Not paying for maintenance (unless specified in the rent agreement).

- Not having the cost of depreciation.

- When you leave for holidays, you can give the car back instead of paying rental during this time.

- Some rental companies include in their prices oil and tire changes.

- Some rental companies cover government taxes for car ownership.

- If you need to leave the country for an unexpected reason, you don't need to rush selling your car for a ridiculous price.

When someone says that paying for car rental is *to lose money for nothing*, often they are forgetting all the reasons above. On various occasions, renting instead of buying is *to save money*.

On the website of my consultancy firm (Colligere Expat Consultancy), you can find a cheat sheet to help calculate what is more beneficial to you. Visit it and do a simulation with your numbers. It might surprise you how renting a car (or use ride-sharing applications) can be more economical.

6 – REVENUE MANAGEMENT IS EVERYWHERE NOW, SO BUY IN ADVANCE

Revenue Management (or RM) is the set of techniques using data and analytics to optimize product availability and price, with the ultimate goal of maximizing revenue. In other words, it is the scientific approach to consumer behaviour regarding price and product offer. Smaller prices when the demand is low, bigger prices when the demand is high (it is not always like that, but this is a good simplification).

This is the reason air ticket prices change so frequently.

RM is also the area I worked during a big part of my career, and airlines are using it for decades already. How each company applies those methods can be the difference between a bankrupt and a profitable carrier.

With techniques developed by some of the greatest airlines in the planet, it was a matter of time until other industries adopt RM for themselves. Nowadays it is in businesses like:

- Hotel and Tourism

- Rail and Bus transportation
- Concerts and Festivals
- Theatres, Stadiums and Sport Events
- Restaurants
- Cinemas

When you see a festival offering cheaper early bird prices, or a cinema charging more for weekend tickets, this is RM. The reason all those industries use *Revenue Management* is that all of them have **a limited number of seats/rooms/tables** to sell, consequently they need to sell it for the ideal price to avoid the flight/show/dinner/movie starting with empty places. You will not see a chocolate company using RM because if they have a period with lower demand for white-chocolate, they will just produce less of it (or make more if the demand is higher).

But why I gave you all this explanation?

To make clear the reason for our hack: As a rule of thumb, and with very few exceptions, RM favours anticipation. Consumers buying tickets earlier allow the company to plan better their future. For this reason, to stimulate early buying, they offer better prices.

If you ever searched for train or bus tickets with DB (Germany), Amtrak (USA), or FlixBus (Europe and USA) you already realized how the prices fluctuate across time. The same happens with major hotel chains.

Notably with touristic packages and hotel rooms, sometimes the best prices will be in the last minute. This allows great opportunities for travellers (as we explained in a previous hack). On the other side, with air tickets, concerts, festivals, and land transportation, it is a safer bet to buy earlier.

7 – HAVE A NEXT VISIT TO HOME BASKET

If you already live abroad, probably there is, somewhere in your room, a pile of random items useless where you live, but essential for your next trip home:

- The keys to your parent's house
- Energy-plug adaptors
- Cash from your home country
- Public transport passes
- Chargers and cables.
- Local documents like health insurance card or driver's license

While not useful at the moment, better not to lose them. You will definitely need them next time you visit your family and friends. To avoid losing it, the best way is to create a small basket or box with everything necessary when travelling back home (or the place that *was* your home).

Remember the hack number 3 of this chapter? This goes in the same line as an extra benefit. When you need to do an emergency trip, those documents, keys, and cash are already together and easy to take to the airport.

8 – NO PUFFY, OR WHY WINDBREAKERS ARE YOUR FRIENDS

The best way to describe those jackets is to think about a middle-term between the Michelin mascot and the *Stay Puft* Marshmallow Man from Ghostbusters. I am talking about these colourful coats that seem to have air trapped inside. They are excellent to keep you warm, even at alpine temperatures, but they have a terrible defect for economical travellers:

They occupy a disproportional part of your baggage allowance!

To make things even more complicated, there is also a second dilemma. Some areas have wide ranges of temperature, depending on factors like altitude or time of the day. If you visit Sochi, host of the 2014 Winter Olympics, you will feel how temperatures in the city can be almost 20 degrees Celsius higher than in the suburbs. The same applies to places like Tehran - and the local altitude variations - or Santiago de Chile, where the daily temperature variations have an incredible range. In the early morning, the weather can be below freezing while at noon is suitable for beach sunbathing (well, not in Tehran). Therefore, the same puffy jacket making you warm and cosy, two hours later feels like a sauna.

How to prepare for this while keeping space in your luggage?

I will summarize the answer in one word: *windbreakers*.

Windbreakers are light jackets made of synthetic material, frequently used by casual runners during the colder season.

To achieve optimal thermal isolation, we should use them with one or two layers of wool (or similar material) sweaters. In this way, you will keep your body warm.

The windbreaker will not allow wind to reach your skin, while the lower layers of wool keep your body temperature and natural warmth. If the temperature increases, just take off one layer or two, until you feel comfortable.

The best part? One windbreaker and two layers of wool-sweaters will take the same or less space than a puffy jacket in your luggage!

With this hack, you are ready for the warm weather of a beach in *Viña del Mar* or to a ski trip in the Andean mountains (hint: if you are in Chile you can do both in the same day).

9 – BE NICE TO THE RECEPTIONISTS

It would shock you to know how much autonomy front-desk agents have in the hospitality industry nowadays. From five-star hotels to no-frills hostels, the epoch when receptionist meant only *key-deliverer* are gone (besides, there are automatic tools for this kind of task, like NFC digital keys).

The receptionist turned into a concierge, a problem-solver, and even a public-relations for many tourism businesses. Since they are the front-line handling service-delivery, management gradually is equipping them with the freedom to make trips memorable and stress-free. The luxury chain The Ritz-Carlton empowers their front-desk agents (and other employees) to spend up to $2000 to delight a guest[112]. You read it right: every receptionist at Ritz can spend up to two thousand dollars to create a memorable experience or to fix a problem for a customer.

While at the hostel I operate in Poland we cannot afford the same budget, our staff is free to do upgrades or give small perks for guests they consider in need of it. For example: If they see a visitor with difficulty to walk, they can offer a ground-level suite even though the client reserved an economical upper-floor room.

In the same way the reception can change you to a better room than the one you reserved, they also can assign a room that they know you will hate. To test this, it is enough to be a jerk with the front-desk agents. Jacob Tomsky, in his book *Heads in Beds: A Reckless Memoir of Hotels, Hustles, and So-Called Hospitality*, recalls how he and his colleagues working in a New York hotel sent guests that were nasty to them to the room 1212. Nothing was wrong with this room, except the fact the phone would ring all night. Since the country and city code of New York is 1212, guests from the hotel would accidentally call this room when trying to make a call without dialling 9 first.

Knowing that receptionists have all this power to make your journey more (or less) pleasant, still surprises me when some people adopt an arrogant and sour posture with those spending night-shifts waiting for your arrival.

Be nice to the reception. First, because they are human and they deserve it. Second, because odds are that eventually your name will be with a friendly remark in their system. When this happens, they will surprise you with free upgrades or welcome drinks.

10 – THE FIRST EXPRESSION YOU SHOULD LEARN IN ANY COUNTRY

There are two types of long-term travellers. The first are those that never learn a single word from the new language surrounding them. They rely only on the fact that people will speak English and, in their minds, there is no need to at least say *Thank You* in the local language.

The second type are the travellers who learn few words (or, for some brave and daring, more than a few). Frequently they begin with the equivalents of *Hello*, *Bye* and *Thank You*. While the importance of those terms is clear, they are far from being the most important thing to learn at first.

To be able to say "Hello" in Russian (*Privet*) possibly will not help to dodge a problem in Russia. Learning how to say *Buenos Dias* ("Good Morning") is nice but unlikely to avoid a confrontation in the public transport of Mexico.

There is one expression to save your skin when you step on someone's foot, or accidentally grab luggage that is not yours in the airport. It is:

I am sorry.

It is beyond belief the number of troubles avoided when you learn how to say that in your new country. I witnessed people enraged in the metro because a passerby accidentally hit them with a bag, realized it, and left without saying sorry. Probably he even didn't know how to say it, but still...

Learn how to say *I am sorry* first. It can be useful already at the immigration when the border guard asks about your room reservation and you realize you forgot to print it.

11 – HOW TO AVOID LOSING MONEY WITH EXCHANGE AND BANK TRANSFERS

During my first long-stay abroad, in 2011, I resorted to traditional bank services, like debit cards, bank transfers and their fees. Commissions bit my money like a wolf dismembering an innocent prey. Fast-forward, from 2017 onwards I gradually abandoned conventional banking to favour cheaper and better services from digital financial institutions, also called *fintechs*.

The first step was to use *Transferwise,* a digital service for international transfers with very favourable exchange rates. The differences are humongous when compared to bank rates, which made this service a weapon of choice for digital nomads everywhere. Later came others like *Azimo* or *Remitly*, each with different innovative characteristics. Still, to this date, *Transferwise* is arguably the leader in international remittances.

Digital transfers give also an additional security. While a normal bank transfer can take days to arrive (depending on the countries of origin and destination), through *Transferwise* sometimes I receive money in less than 24 hours. Therefore, for an emergency, you can reach the needed resources sooner than later.

I also adopted a digital wallet, namely *Skrill*. The major competitor of *Skrill* is PayPal, the financial behemoth and pioneer in this area. The reason I favoured the first instead of the second is the bureaucracy of PayPal in some services, which reminds me of usual banks.

At last, I closed my Brazilian bank account (which was costing me roughly 5 dollars per month, for nothing) and opened an account in a digital bank, free of charge.

All these changes together save less than a dozen euros per month. However, in the long term, this is a considerable amount. The additional benefit of faster transactions and the availability everywhere make payments a piece of cake.

With all the benefits, there are two essential things you should take care of before going digital with your finances. The first is to have a safe internet connection. The second is to be aware that *fintechs* are often more fragile than big, traditional banks. Therefore, do not concentrate all your resources in a single place otherwise, in an economical crash, you will be on risky ground.

12 – THE BEST TOOL TO NOT FORGET YOUR NATIVE LANGUAGE

If you are planning to live abroad for just a year or less, this advice will not be notably useful for you. It is unlikely that in such a short period you will forget much of your language or lose your grammatical skills. Yes, we all know that guy who spent the summer in France and came back saying *Merci* instead of *Thank you* and later apologizes for the confusion. However, I think most of those are fake, made up just to look sophisticated (but end up looking silly).

However, if you are planning to stay a longer period far away and with limited contact with your native language, there is a real chance your linguistic skills will decrease.

The worst part?

This decrease speeds up over time and affects all dimensions: reading, writing, and even your accent!

Regular conversations with your parents and friends help to not forget the pronunciation of certain words, but still the way you speak will change. The tonus of your tongue muscles will change. My native language, Brazilian Portuguese, is spoken with very open vowels and not many *sheesh* sounds (those made with the tongue between the teeth). Polish is completely the opposite. It is almost like the first sounds like a vacuum cleaner and the second like the opening of a soda can. The usage of Polish on a day-to-day basis affects how I pronounce Portuguese. People notice it.

While the differences in your accents will only be a reason for laughs, it will not make you look stupid. The real problem comes when your orthography and grammar decline.

I realized it when I forgot how to write *tea* in Portuguese (*chá*). I wrote *Xá,* and this was enough for the general surprise in an internet group discussion with friends. So, I decided it was time to work on the maintenance of my mother language. While I could train my talking and listening skills by speaking to my relatives, my reading and writing skills would require me to read (and write) more. But there was another obstacle:

Where in Poland could I find books in Portuguese?

That is when I resorted to an e-book reader. Probably the best investment I did in that year. Not only the books were cheaper and instantly available, it was also very comfortable to carry, plus the *e-ink* screen doesn't hurt my eyes. In the following year, I broke my personal record and read over 30 books, because I was taking this little black gadget everywhere with me. I was reading in the public transport on my way to work, or on the train during my weekend trips.

My vocabulary improved drastically, and I got closer to my fatherland culture. Every Brazilian book I read made me feel near the place I came from.

My e-book reader broke after more than a year when I accidentally dropped it from a table. Still, the number of books read on it paid for itself, so I bought another one.

Besides all benefits of keeping your native language and practising new idioms that you are learning, there is an additional personal enhancement. Maybe even more important than any other:

Amplifying your cultural growth.

13 – YOU DON'T NEED TO CARRY YOUR LUGGAGE EVERYWHERE

Digital nomads know this feeling: You are leaving temporarily your hotel or hostel and going to another city for a few weeks, but do not have a place to your luggage until you return. To carry everything with you is too expensive. Either you need to rent a costly (or distant) storage room, or pay a fee to the reception to keep it.

There are two ways to tackle this problem.

The first is suitable for situations where you are leaving for a few days and need a safe place for your stuff. The solution lies in applications like *Stasher* or *BagBnb.*

Those services will help you find spaces in hotels, stores, or convention centres to leave your things safely while paying reasonable prices. With those apps, in some European capitals you can store your bag for five euros or less per day.

If you are travelling somewhere with a low-cost airline that charges 50 euros to dispatch one piece of luggage, maybe will be cheaper to use this solution instead of carrying everything with you.

The second method is suitable for situations where you are moving permanently and is straightforward:

Travel light, even when you are travelling for long periods. You don't need to pack like you are going to a post-apocalyptic land. Force yourself to be a minimalist.

I lived in the Middle East for almost three years. Still, when moving out, my total dispatched luggage was virtually the same as when I arrived: two 23 kg bags. In the two bags, I had everything I needed to move to Europe after three years living there.

How was it possible? The first is explanation is that I always rented furnished apartments, therefore I never needed to carry heavy furniture or accessories from one country to the next one. The second is that I just sold everything too big, heavy or costly to move, like:

- Sound system
- Kitchenware like pans, pots, and cutlery
- Technical books I did not need anymore.
- Racks and cloth hangers

To transport those items would be more expensive than to just sell it and buy it again at my new home. Selling was easy, particularly with so many groups in social media to announce used stuff.

The additional benefit of travelling light and knowing solutions like *Stasher* is that, for an emergency, you can leave the country quicker since you are not carrying much. This happened with thousands of digital nomads and expats at the moment I write this book, during the COVID-19 crisis.

14 – HOW TO PAY LESS AT AIRBNB

Most Ho(s)teliers (I am one of them) dislike websites like *Expedia* - intermediaries between the guest and the ho(s)tel. The reason is they offer terrible support for the properties and take a considerable share of the price you pay for accommodation. Most sites charge around 15% commission. This means that from a 100 dollars reservation, the property will receive only 85 dollars for providing all the hospitality you experience plus paying for the water, heating, and employees. Meanwhile, *Expedia* (or other portals) receives 15 dollars, their prize to offer nothing besides poor customer service.

Unfortunately, we - hotel and hostel owners - cannot live without those sites, because they drive a considerable share of our clients. On the other side, every ho(s)telier have a favourite (or less-disliked) accommodation portal.

My (and for many others) is *Airbnb*. There are two reasons to prefer them.

First: they charge the property only 3% commission. Therefore, from the same reservation of 100 dollars mentioned before, the amount to the property will be $97. The trick is that Airbnb also charges a commission from the guests; therefore, they can relieve the properties. Eventually, those 3% commissions instead of 15% make a big difference for any hotel.

The second reason is the evaluation system. Most portals allow the guest to review the hotel. This is fine, since it creates accountability for the accommodation provider. Regrettably, this is a one-sided system, since the Hotel cannot review the client and a terrible guest (like those stealing items or rude with receptionists) goes unpunished. *Airbnb* at this point is different and allows both sides to review each other. The result is that the guests *Airbnb* send to us are usually more pleasant and easy-going.

But where is the hack until now?

Here it is: You can ask for an additional discount when you find an *Airbnb* announcement interesting to you. Go to the same screen used to communicate with the accommodation. Instead of clicking *Request to Book*, click *Contact this host* and put your stay dates. The provider can offer you a tailor-made price.

Naturally, given the fact Airbnb charges less commission from the ho(s)tels and has a better evaluation system, there is a chance they (or we, since I am also a hostel manager) will give you an extra discount.

Maybe when other fellow hostel owners read this hack, they will hate me (sorry for that!), therefore I recommend to you to use this tip with caution and respectfully.

15 – APPOINTMENTS YOU MUST DO BEFORE LEAVING

Once a friend of mine from the health sector explained to me how important is access to the past information of a patient. By past, he meant previous exam results, diagnostics and similar information. The world-renowned Cleveland Clinic affirms it in their *HealthEssential* page[13]:

When doctors treat you for years, they get to know your medical history inside and out. That helps them make accurate diagnoses, watch for red flags regarding medications and monitor changes in your health through the years. But the "family" in family doctor matters, too. Seeing multiple generations of a family can help a doctor record an accurate, in-depth family health history. For example, if I know you had cancer at a young age, and so did your mother, that's a red flag.

For this reason, even if you are moving to a country with universal healthcare services like Canada or the UK, it is wise to make an appointment with your local doctor and dentist.

This is especially critical if your destination is a place with exorbitant medical costs (yes, I am looking to you, USA). Nobody enjoys unpleasant news from health specialists, but you will prefer to know if there is any problem before you move out and before you need to use your international health insurance.

In my family country, dentist prices are smaller than in Europe. For this reason, when I visit my parents, even for a short time, I try to schedule a visit to the dentist. He can do small repairs and warns me is something is not going right.

Schedule a visit to your local dentist, a medical checkup, and a blood exam. Look if your vaccination card is up to date. Those things may not be the most amusing part of a travel plan, but it can save money and even your life.

16 – RESEARCH YOUR PRESCRIPTION PRICES

There is almost nothing in my native country, Brazil, that is cheaper than abroad. Electronics or wine cost more than nearly anywhere else. The only place where I found worse prices for alcohol were in the Middle East, because of the *sin tax* on drinks. There is, however, one product relatively cheap in Brazil:

Drugs.

I mean, pharmaceutical drugs.

The reason is that, years ago, the government stimulated the development of national labs producing medicines with broken patents, called *Genéricos*. A *Genérico* doesn't have a brand name, you buy it by the active ingredient. The most important thing: It may cost less than half the price of its branded counterpart.

I take one of those *genéricos*, called *Finasteride*. It avoids hair fall and Hollywood celebrities already know it for some time (like Bradley Cooper[1]). In Brazil, the monthly cost of taking finasteride was around 30 reais. Roughly 8 dollars at that time. When I moved to Poland, I forgot to check the price before boarding the plane. I took my 1-month box with me, my prescription (since it needs one) and moved to Europe.

After the first month, I needed to buy more. If you stop taking finasteride, your hair falls again. In Poland, there are no *genér-*

icos and finasteride is available with the name *Propecia* (the same as in other markets like the USA).

In 2020, the cost for 1 month of treatment is (hold your seat): 180zl. 43 dollars. Over five times the Brazilian price.

I stopped taking it, and my hair started to fall. Fortunately, I had a trip scheduled to Brazil a few months later. After a visit to my dermatologist, he made a prescription of finasteride as a continuous usage drug, allowing me to buy and take with me to Europe many more boxes.

I still have my curly and black as an obsidian hair over my head. Victory.

Concluding the lesson:
1. Before moving out, check the destination prices of all (legal) drugs that you need.
2. If needed or requested by the destination laws, visit your doctor for a prescription.
3. Translate the prescription with a sworn translator. If the airport security checks you, this will come in handy. Otherwise, you risk being mistaken for an amphetamine dealer or similar.

17 – THE HACK TO REMEMBER YOUR PASSWORDS

Any person who is not *off the grid* often has dozens of passwords. For digital nomads, expats and travellers the situation is worse, since every residence change can double the number of passwords you need to retrieve. At some point, you will need to remember the passwords of your local bank and original bank, of the website used for freelance gigs and of your personal and business email, and there it goes.

To remember all of them is a tremendous challenge. To solve this problem, some people resort to a very **dangerous** solution:

Have the same password for multiple sites. Or even worse: Have the same for multiple sites **and** their emails!

Your email is the biggest backdoor you have. If a hacker gets access to it, he can steal your personal information and gain access to your accounts. Remember all the buttons *Click here if you forgot your PIN* in the websites you use every day? Most of them just will send the password to your email. If a hacker has access to your email, they will have **everything.**

I hope that at this point you are aware of the importance of not repeating the same key everywhere. So, now comes the second challenge: How to remember everything?

To just write in an Excel list or notepad document is a bad idea. For the same reason above: it is the first thing a hacker will look for when invading a computer, and it will not be difficult to find it.

There are two remaining ways:

The first, my favourite, is to write it on a piece of paper and leave it in an accessible place only for you. This is something that a hacker cannot steal, because he can invade your hard disk but not your drawer. For safety purposes, it is even better to write in 2 or 3 places and leave all of them in different locations. If something happens with the paper in your drawer, there are still the others. The biggest problem of this method is that every time you update a password, you need to rewrite each paper.

The second is to use an app to keep your passwords and use if you forget it. There are many options available, like KeePassX, LastPass, Dashlane, Keeper, SplashID and 1Password. Some of those apps will store your passwords and ask you to create an additional PIN to access them. The downsides here are two: first is that most of those apps are paid, and second is if you lose the PIN to access the app, you lost *all* your passwords at once.

Both ways are much better than putting the same pass everywhere or having your account locked because you forgot what secret word you chose.

18 – THE HACK TO NOT PAY FOR EXCESS LUGGAGE

In one of my previous hacks, I wrote about ways to travel light. Still, sometimes it is not possible. Sometimes we carry a lot of stuff because we will be longer in a place where we need certain items (like your vinyl's if you are an old-school DJ).

Some people opt to pay the airline's excess baggage charges. In Europe, this is around 60 euros per 23 kg bag[lxi], while in American Airlines it costs whooping 150 dollars[lxii].

If you think this amount is not a problem, I bet you are either transporting something extremely valuable and necessary, or probably your bank account has many more 0s than mine. For those that prefer to pay less and wait a few days more, there are great options. Options that will cost less than what airlines charge. They also cost less than traditional delivery companies like FedEx or UPS. Still, for some reason, many people don't know about it.

I am talking about 3 shipment services providers:

- *Eurosender*, which works across most European countries.

- *Lugless*, available in the United States

- *Luggage Forward*, operating in countries all over the world (and likely more expensive than those above).

Those services are not usual transportation companies, but rather platforms connecting customers (individuals and companies) looking for a logistic provider. Something like *Uber*, but for baggage. With Eurosender, you can send a bag to another European country for 20 euros. Lugless, inside the United States, have similar rates.

What to do with all the money you will save in airline fees? I suggest buying my other book, which complements this one: *Moving Out, Living Abroad and Keeping your Sanity*. A *thank you* is also fine!

19 – PASSIVE INCOME RENTING YOUR OLD PLACE

The title of this hack is, apparently, contradictory. How a Digital *Nomad* can rent his home? Does a nomad even have a home?

Let's talk about one common situation among those living abroad: the *breaks*. The *long breaks*. Commonly, expatriates and nomads visit their native countries. Be it to visit family and friends, holidays or to do the essential checks I explained in previous hacks.

If you live in a Hostel or B&B, you probably will just finish your reservation in the day of your departure and stop paying for a room you will not use. However, if you are living in an apartment or renting a room, you cannot put your contract on hold for weeks (or months), when you are out.

Now imagine: You will be out for 3 weeks. If you live in an eastern European capital, like me, the price of a room per week is about 200 dollars (185 euros), in an ordinary location. For an apartment is much more. If you are staying 3 weeks out, it means by leaving your apartment empty; you are leaving at the table $600!

This would pay about half of the plane ticket to visit my family and back!

Some people may worry about strangers sleeping in your bed. But just as I stated before, the review system of Airbnb ensures most guests behave well. For the few that don't, the website has an insurance up to 1 million dollars to pay for the damage caused by bad visitors.

Some guests even leave behind gifts for their hosts. ☺

20 - FORECAST YOUR LIVING COSTS

I always use two versatile cost-comparing websites since moved out from my country almost a decade ago. Numbeo[117] and Expatistan[118]. Those sites use the concept of user-generated content and online collaboration to create massive databases of consumer prices:

- Food, including stuff like 12 eggs, 1 litre of milk or a combo meal in a fast-food restaurant.

- Housing, with details like rent in both expensive and normal areas, and utilities.

- Clothes

- Transportation: Price of gasoline, monthly transport ticket, taxi trip, etc.

- Personal Care: Medicines, deodorant, shampoo, etc.

- Entertainment

Users input in those websites the item price for their locations. With the growing number of consultations, the tool gains greater precision. *Numbeo* has over 6 million values divided between almost ten thousand cities on the planet. In *Expatistan* you can consult the cost of living of over 2 thousand cities.

Using those tools I can verify that my previous city, Doha, is 99% more expensive than my current one, Warsaw. (This goes in line with my memories of paying unrealistic prices for a beer).

With this load of information, it is easy to compare living costs in your new destination and former country. It will be possible to discover if you will survive in a strict budget, live normally or have *pesos* enough for a lavish lifestyle.

21 – NEW ALTERNATIVES TO PROTECT YOURSELF

Do you know someone who had acute appendicitis? It starts with a sudden pain in your abs. The development is quick and brutal. If treatment (frequently surgical) is not available immediately, the patient life can be at risk.

This is just an example of the many complications possible while you are in Bali, Chiang Mai or Lima.

It can happen to everyone. I also had a complication one time, although not as unexpected as appendicitis: an accident while practising downhill skiing. I did not have insurance for risky sports, so the hospital bill emptied my bank account.

When we talk about travel and health insurance, maybe the first names coming to your mind are giants like Allianz, Amex or AXA (Is there some hidden rule about insurance companies starting with the letter A?). Those multinationals have packages to a wide public range, from families to seniors. However, they often penalize travellers like digital nomads, or at least do not offer the most convenient (and price-wise) option for those travelling for longer terms.

For this reason, recently there was a surge of online companies offering insurance services according to the needs of expatriates and long-term travellers. Some examples are:

- *Safety Wings*, offering services for international nomads and remote professionals.

- *World Nomads*, offering coverage to a wide range of activities like Bungee Jumping, Scuba Diving and Skiing. If I had their insurance, I would not need to pay a small fortune after my accident.

- *International Insurance.com*, which partners with Cigna Global Medical Health to offer tailor-made solutions for expatriates.

The biggest difference from those companies to traditional insurance is that their products take into consideration *digital nomads* and *expats*. For this reason, they have convenient prices, ideal coverage to the activity level of young professionals, and geographical flexibility.

22 - THE PERFECT TIME TO LOOK FOR HOUSING

Rent prices are not the same over the entire year. Therefore, before start explaining, I have a short disclaimer to do:

This entire subchapter is considering the seasons of the Northern Hemisphere, more specifically the USA and Europe. If your place is below the equator line, remember that our winter is your summer and vice versa. The same applies to the end of the school year.

Having said this, there are some interesting data to share:

In 2019, the portal Renthop researched real estate rent in 10 major American cities[19]. It concluded that the best time to look for a roof was either November (in 1 city), December (6 cities) or January (2 cities). The only exception was Chicago, where the cheapest month is March. So, in 90% of the places researched, the most favourable time of the year is winter, when the rent can be close to $140 cheaper!

In Europe, the situation is similar. The website Movebubble pointed out that in London, the months with the lowest demand for rentals are also from November to January[20].

Some reasons for winter being the cheapest season are:

- There is no demand coming from new students, like at the beginning of the school year.

- There is no demand from recently graduated, moving to metropolitan areas after finishing their studies, like in the summer.

- People changing jobs and leaving their homes, like other unexpected vacancies, happen year-round, but there is little or no new tenants to replace them in the winter.

For other parts of the world, you can find the best month to rent in property portals like GlobalPropertyGuide[21].

Bottom line: if you are moving to Europe or North America (and don't mind carrying your things in freezing weather), better wait until winter.

23 – KITCHEN SUBSTITUTES

This is a common complaint I hear from my fellow Brazilian expats. In fact, this is a usual protest made by all those expatriates from countries with exotic cuisines:

I cannot cook X, or Y, or Z because it is impossible to find any suitable ingredient here!

It is comprehensible. A Brazilian living in Eastern Europe would crave for *Pão de Queijo* if he sees a picture of his friends eating it at the local bakery. A central-European Slavic would miss his *żurek / kyselo / kisyalitsa* (all of them are fermented cereal soups, respectively from Poland, Czech and Belarus) if he lived in South America.

It is because is difficult to find the proper ingredients for such recipes. But it is still possible to do them.

Here is a secret I will tell you: there is a website that shows you the substitutes for almost any exotic ingredient. Substitutes available in the part of the world where you are living.

This website is Wikipedia.

But first, you must use it differently from what is usual. The first step is entering Wikipedia in your native language. There you search for the ingredient you are looking for. Once on its page, look at the left bar, where is an option to see the same page in different languages.

Voilà!

By doing this you will discover, for example, that to do Pao de Queijo you need something called *Polvilho*. It is near impossible to find this in Eastern Europe, but you can easily substitute it for Tapioca flour (in fact, both *Polvilho* and Tapioca flour comes from the same vegetable, Cassava).

My wife made Pão de Queijo with this substitute. It was great.

Really great.

Remember the Wikipedia trick the next time you are looking to do a home recipe. *Bon Appétit!*

24 – THE TRAVEL COMBO YOU ARE NOT USING

Maybe you realized how competitive is the travel market. Pay attention to the colossal amount of *pop-ups*, announcements and billboards sponsored by airlines, travel companies and hotel chains, both on the internet and real life. All of them want a piece of your next holiday savings. Until recently, the two most valuable football teams in the planet were sponsored by competing airlines (Real Madrid by Emirates and Barcelona by Qatar Airways).

That is why it is **getting common** non-competing companies joining forces to create **better deals** (and marketing campaigns). The last time I was booking a flight with a Turkish airline, they offered me very good discounts if I also reserved a hotel in my destination with them. On top of that, they even would credit me some extra miles. I took the deal.

Before I start with the advantages of those bundles, a disclaimer: is not all roses.

If you need flexibility, booking everything together is not for you. To change a flight *or* a Hotel when they are bundled together in a promotion may cause heavier penalties.

Here are a few Pros of reserving airline+hotel combos.

- The prices frequently are lower than reserving separately hotel and air-tickets.

- You may earn extra miles in the airline frequent flyer program.

- Global carriers will rarely partner with substandard hotels. While **working in an airline, I had a colleague whose job was to travel the world and check if the affiliated hotels were good enough.** *That was a sweet job.*

- Especially for last-minute travel, you can save a considerable amount. *See also our hack about Last-Minute travel in the first part of this book.*

- During high-season, the prices of air tickets and hotel reservations vary wildly. It is difficult to match the time when airlines and hotels offer their best prices. This is not a problem when you buy a package containing both.

So, the next time you book a flight and a dialogue box at the airline site asks if you would like to reserve a hotel too, check if the benefits are good. Sometimes it is.

25 – THE EXTRA PILLOWCASE

I almost started this paragraph saying that this is a *Bear Grylls*-level hack, but there is no advice to drink your own pee. Therefore, let's just say this is a pro-level survival skill for everyone used to long airport layovers.

Take an extra pillowcase in your hand-luggage. You will not regret it.

In Europe, over one in every five flights are delayed[22]. In other parts of the world, unpunctuality happens too. Unless you are at an airport with very comfortable chairs (like HIA in Doha), or your credit card gives you complimentary entrances to the VIP lounge, you will thank me for this advice.

Possibly the worst part of getting stranded during long hours is to not have a place to rest your head. Even if you are lucky enough to find a row of chairs without the fixed arm-rest to lay horizontally. You crave for a pillow, but with restricted luggage allowances, seldom somebody carries one. Conversely, a pillowcase occupies minimal space.

You can stuff the extra pillow case with shirts or sweaters and turn it in an improvised (and comfortable) place to lean your head. Now you will only miss the free alcohol of the VIP lounge.

26 – THE HACK TO KEEP YOUR STUFF ALWAYS SMELLING FRESH

A single used shirt.

A lone underwear.

A simple pair of socks after an afternoon sightseeing.

Those are some things that can make your once flawless, organized, lavender-scented luggage smell like a gym bag. One piece of stinky cloth is enough to make your once perfumed and unblemished attires, carefully chosen for tonight's party, smell like the uniform of a quarry worker (at the end of his shift).

There is one way to minimize this and one definitive solution for it.

To reduce this problem, try to avoid synthetic materials. Cotton, wool and other natural fibres are not odorous as polyester, for example.

Additionally, I carry plastic bags inside my luggage to pack separately used clothes (especially socks and shoes), but after a long period, the smell leaks out of it. The definitive solution is simple, but unknown for so many experienced travellers:

Dryer sheets

They are on the market for a long time, since the middle of the last century, helping people to keep their clothes dry and soft. Most of the varieties today have scents, so it is a guarantee of fresh-smell.

Hence, put a dryer sheet close to the dirty clothes in your luggage. Just be aware that if the fragrance is too strong, it can smell too chemical. Natural alternatives are wooden drying balls or cedar chips, which will also reduce the humidity inside.

With this trick, the unpleasant smell of your used clothes will not transfer to the clean ones.

If you want to meet interesting people, share drinks and not be ignored when asking for information, smelling good is an excellent first step.

27 – YOU ONLY NEED ONE UNIVERSAL ADAPTER

I am a big fan of different cuisines, sports and music.

What I am not a fan is of different energy plugs. Currently, there are 15 main types in the world, and there is not one truly universal. The electrical plug of my country, Brazil, is the same of South Africa. Meanwhile the one I used in the Middle East is the British standard. In Poland, they differ from both previously mentioned countries.

If you are planning a long trip, you may feel tempted to buy in advance all the adapters needed. You may also think about buying more than one of each plug. Otherwise, how could you charge a phone and a laptop at the same time, right?

Wrong.

You don't need to buy multiple adapters. You need only one. If you look for a *World Travel Adapter,* you will find it. They look slightly bulkier than the normal adapters and their shape is convertible using small buttons. In this way, they fit almost all kinds of electrical sockets. This adapter is more expensive than a normal one, but by being useful in the entire world, it is investment-worthy.

One question remains: Should I buy multiple units of those *World Travel Adapters*?

No. You only need one of them and one power strip with few energy sockets. In this way, you use the adapter to plug the power strip and charge your electronics in the slots of the strip.

Besides having enough energy for all your gadgets, you can be the hero of the Hostel by allowing others to charge in your strip.

28 – THE HACK TO HELP YOU NEVER LOSE YOUR MEMORIES

One thing I seek to deliver to the clients of my consulting company[23] is peace of mind. Sometimes, to achieve that is challenging, like when you are moving abroad and have intricate doubts about immigration procedures. However, often our peace of mind is just one USB plug away. I am telling you this because there is a method to save things significant for you, and simultaneously, protect:

- All your travel pictures
- Family videos.
- Scan of important documents.
- Your portfolio or work material (if you are a digital nomad).

If you never had your phone stolen in the last days of a trip (together with all the pictures) or had a computer dead after falling from your desk, consider yourself lucky. Chances are something similar will happen at some point. When the moment comes, you will ask yourself:

Why I never made a backup? How could I be so foolish!?

When leaving my country, in 2013, one of the first things I bought was a 500 GB SSD external drive. I knew that living abroad and travelling constantly, a stolen or lost luggage could result in losing all my documents and pictures. I still have this SSD drive to back up my documents one time per week, every week.

Although I bought it such a long time ago, the SSD technology still guarantees fast and seamless transfer. The few minutes spent doing backups are a small cost for the peace of mind of having my documents safe.

It is important to remember: do not put your backup drive together with your laptop and phone, because if you lose one, you lose all of them. It always should be in a different and safer place.

The tech-savvy reader may ask why I don't store my backup *in the cloud*. This is a good question, but there are two issues with using cloud technology to back up personal documents:

1. It can take more time or even become unavailable, depending on the connection quality and accessibility of the cloud storage. If there is no internet connection, you cannot retrieve the backup.
2. You are entrusting an immense amount of personal data and documents to a third party. During frequent data leaks, unknown surveillance and personal info used for marketing purposes without consent, this is not only risky but a shot in the dark.

No matter which type of backup system you prefer, SSD drive or cloud storage, to have one will help you not worry about lost pictures the next time someone steals your phone.

29 – DO NOT PUT YOUR (AND YOUR CLIENT) CREDIT CARD AT RISK

At the very beginning of this book, I wrote a useful and money-saving hack with VPNs: to use them to buy flight tickets. But if you think the convenience of a VPN is limited to pre-travel preparation, better keep reading.

When moving out, especially if staying in temporary rooms, B&Bs or Apart-hotels until finding a definite place, frequently you will need to use public Wi-Fi networks. There is nothing wrong with them if you are using it to read a blog or watch TV series, since in some countries like Lithuania[24] they can be incredibly fast.

However, frequently expats and digital nomads use the internet for purposes involving their bank accounts, payments and other financial purposes. Or even worse: transmission of classified customer information. To transfer such important data relying on the security of a public network is not only irresponsible but (in many countries), illegal. If a hacker finds a backdoor to your computer through a public connection and steals credit card information of your clients, you can be liable for eventual losses.

One of the first steps is obvious but not always possible: do not use public networks to transmit sensitive information.

Yet, we know we must do some things at an exact moment and cannot wait until you find a safe connection. For such situations, there are two possibilities:

1. Use the *tethering* function of your phone to share the mobile connection with your computer. Unfortunately, it can quickly consume your data package and it is not rare that telecommunication companies charge extra for using this function, like Verizon[25].
2. Subscribe to a VPN service provider. VPNs, which stands for *Virtual Private Network*, especially those paid ones, will mask your data under a sub-network protected by password and (usually) encrypted transmission.

The internet-security blog *Pixelprivacy* explains how a VPN works to protect you in the following words[26]:

A Virtual Private Network (VPN) is arguably the best way to encrypt your internet traffic - all of your internet traffic.

A VPN encases your internet connection in a layer of encryption. This prevents third parties from monitoring your online travels. While they can tell you're connected to the internet, they can't tell what websites or other services you've accessed.

The monthly price of a VPN subscription can be less than 10 USD[27]. If you are handling private information and payments (personal or for customers), this is a small price to pay to pump up your cyber security.

30 – SAVE YOUR NECK

The last hack of this book is probably the easiest to apply. So you should do it immediately (and motivate yourself to apply the other hacks earlier in the list).

Most expats and virtually all digital nomads use laptops for their work. While laptops give you the benefit of mobility, they have a serious ergonomic problem: the lower height of their screens force you to look down while using them. You may not realize, but this constant effort is damaging your back, shoulders and **productivity**. You get tired faster when forced to an unnatural position, like looking down.

I accidentally discovered how helpful a stand is for those situations. My notebook was overheating while running heavy software, so I looked for a stand with extra fans to cool it down. Besides the desired effect of my laptop not melting, it also made the usage of it more comfortable. Before I needed to have short breaks all the time because of neck discomfort, but now (literally right now, while I am writing this book), I can sit and work during hours feeling no pain.

So, some benefits of having a laptop stand are:

- It will avoid neck, back and shoulder pain

- If the stand has some extra fans, it will cool your computer and improve its performance when demanded.

- It will raise productivity and permit you to work longer without soreness.

- It can be ergonomic for your wrists.

- Some more sophisticated versions have extra features, like additional USB ports.

On top of all this, they are inexpensive, with entry versions priced around 15 USD. Your increase in productivity can quickly return the investment.

[28]*Source of the image: Colegio de la Esperanza*

RESOURCES TO MAKE YOUR LIFE ABROAD EASIER

To learn the language and the culture: Some people are used to language apps like Duolingo. On the other side, I am passionate about Lingq because of their extremely friendly interface, the user community where everyone helps each other correcting exercises and the possibility of importing books, articles and songs to the app. You can use it to learn a new idiom and immerse in its culture simultaneously. Using it I reached a conversational level in one of the hardest European languages, Polish, without going to any formal course.

You can check Lingq by clicking here.

To transfer money between your old and new country: This recommendation saved me once when just after arriving, I realized I miscalculated the amount of money to bring. To do a normal international transfer would mean lose with bad exchange rates. Transferwise have rates that are much better than most banks, and their transfers may take less than 24 hours.

Create your account using this link and win $20 in your first transfer: http://bit.ly/2TVU0vZ

To not confuse currencies or overspend: XE currency converter is both a website and a mobile app easy to use and updated in real-time. Available at: https://www.xe.com/currencyconverter/

To find a quick loo, anywhere: It will take a while until knowing where are the public bathrooms in your new place. Meanwhile, you can use Flush, an app available to Android and Apple mobiles with a catalogue of thousands of public toilets. Download it at Google Play Store in http://bit.ly/2TRhUIZ (available also at Apple Store).

To compare the cost of living: There are two websites, each with millions of prices in their databases, essential to estimate if your salary will be enough to make the ends meet. They are Numbeo (https://www.numbeo.com/) and Expatistan (https://www.expatistan.com/)

To rent your former house or apartment and make extra cash: When we move out not completely sure if we will come back, or have no time to find a tenant/sell our property, a good solution is to make it available at Airbnb for short-term rental. They even have tools to manage the property remotely and handle things like cleaning and insurance. It is not rare that people make twice the amount of cash on Airbnb compared to what they would earn if they just rented it for a single tenant.

You can check the option of becoming an Airbnb Host through this link (and earn an awesome gift from them): https://www.airbnb.com/x/jonataslevib

To be updated about the most cutting-edge tips and tricks for expats, digital nomads and long-term travellers: The blog of my consultancy firm, where I share weekly insights of life overseas.

https://expatriateconsultancy.com/digital-nomads-expats-and-travellers-blog/

DID YOU ENJOY THIS BOOK?

The best award I could have is your opinion! I would be glad to read your thoughts on this book in a review on Goodreads and Amazon.

I invite you to visit the page of my consultancy, Colligere Expat Consultancy, with weekly updates and valuable tips. There you will find the modern methods for travellers & expats save money, increase productivity and boost their quality of life.

www.expatriateconsultancy.com

Last but not least, we can keep in contact through my page:

Levi Borba - Digital Nomad & Expat mentoring

www.facebook.com/leviporai

Or via my Medium page:

https://leviborba.medium.com/

FROM THE SAME AUTHOR

Moving Out, Working Abroad and Keeping Your Sanity: 11 secrets to make your expat life better than you imagine

- **The most decisive expert for your success abroad and how to have free access to him.**
- The advice for your family you will never regret following. Neither they will.
- How to adapt to the local behaviours and etiquette in a matter of days.
- **How to thrive like a native without being one.**

Buy it on Amazon here: https://www.amazon.com/dp/B084GF14CZ

Starting Your Own Business Far From Home: What (Not) to Do When Opening a Company in Another State, Country, or Galaxy (The Digital Nomad & Expat Mentor Book 3)

★ **The Business and Non-Business factors to consider when choosing a place to open a company.** *Often neglected, they are the difference between catastrophic failures and remarkable success.*

★ How to find local allies

★ How to understand your competition better than themselves!

★ How to discover and avoid paths leading to business destruction.

★ How to absorb environmental changes and use them in your favor. (Hint: Taleb).

★ **What should you know to not be fooled (avoid the mistakes we made).**

Buy it in Amazon, here: https://www.amazon.com/dp/B08L1G1D1Q

ABOUT THE AUTHOR

With the knowledge gathered by living and travelling to over 50 countries, Levi Borba wrote the book that became one of the business travel bestsellers in Amazon: *Moving Out, Living Abroad and Keeping your Sanity*.

He is also the co-founder of **Nearby Airport Hostel Warsaw** and **Hotelik&Parking Okecie 39**. After finishing studies at the University of São Paulo (USP), he was admitted to one of the fiercest management trainee programs in Latin America. There, he spent a year mentored by high-level executives. He moved to Chile and later to Qatar to join the team of the best airline that humankind has ever created. After years of development, he moved to Europe to take his dreams from paper and started an entrepreneurial project in the hospitality sector.

In 2020, Levi Borba started a new venture, **Colligere Expat Consultancy** to help expats and digital nomads have a seamless, stress-free experience abroad and overcome bureaucracy.

ENDNOTES

[1] Information about Claim Compass and how to be compensated by problems with your airline ticket can be checked in this referral link: https://www.claimcompass.eu/ref/colligere-expat-consultancy

[2] You can check this service at the Turkish Airlines website: https://www.turkishairlines.com/en-us/flights/hotel-service/

[3] https://www.tui.pl/last-minute

[4] https://www.lufthansaholidays.com/en-de/last-minute

[5] https://www.wakacje.pl/lastminute/

[6] https://www.thelocal.it/20170420/teenager-fined-10000-for-public-peeing-in-italy

[7] https://www.businessinsider.com/flushing-toilet-seat-up-sprays-water-germs-2016-3?IR=T

[8] You can try Lingq to ramp up the speed of your language learning at this link: http://bit.ly/36qzd6n

[9] It means *wonderful* in Polish.

[10] Visit the content-rich blog for travellers, expats and digital nomads of my consultancy here: http://expatriateconsultancy.com/digital-nomads-expats-and-travellers-blog/

[11] The Rental vs Purchasing a car and many

other useful pieces of information for expats and digital nomads are at the blog of Colligere Expat Consultancy: http://expatriateconsultancy.com/digital-nomads-expats-and-travellers-blog/

[12] You can learn more about the employee empowerment philosophy of Ritz Carlton here: https://realbusiness.co.uk/the-ritz-carlton-effect-why-businesses-need-to-empower-employees/

[13] https://health.clevelandclinic.org/5-reasons-you-should-have-a-family-doctor/

[14] https://www.dailymail.co.uk/tvshowbiz/article-2563116/Bradley-Cooper-taking-Propecia-preventative-baldness-therapy-sources-claim.html

[15] https://upgradedpoints.com/lufthansa-baggage-fees/

[16] https://www.lugless.com/airline-baggage-fees/american-airlines-baggage-fees/

[17] https://www.numbeo.com/cost-of-living/

[18] https://www.expatistan.com/cost-of-living/comparison/

[19] https://www.renthop.com/studies/national/best-time-of-year-to-rent

[20] https://www.movebubble.com/renterhub/best-time-of-year-to-find-a-new-rental-home-london

[21] https://www.globalpropertyguide.com

[22] https://skift.com/2019/06/28/europe-still-has-a-

shocking-number-of-flight-delays/

[23] You can find us here: http://expatriateconsultancy.com/

[24] *Top 20 Countries w/ the Fastest Public WiFi* https://pointmetotheplane.boardingarea.com/top-20-countries-w-fastest-public-wifi/

[25] *Does VZW charge for tethering? (It's been a while)* https://www.reddit.com/r/verizon/comments/4jth3m/does_vzw_charge_for_tethering_its_been_a_while/

[26] *How To Encrypt Your Internet Traffic* https://pixelprivacy.com/resources/how-to-encrypt-your-traffic/

[27] *How Much Does a VPN Solution Cost?* https://www.avoxi.com/blog/vpn-solution-cost/

[28] https://www.colegiodelaesperanza.com/la-influencia-de-maestros-y-padres-en-la-higiene-postural-en-el-colegio-y-en-casa/

133